Fabulous
Life of our Saints

Fabulous is a collection of Elementary School books aimed at having a direct impact on Catholic Saints awareness for kids.

Our Full Collection is also available via Amazon:

SCAN ME

Scan here!
Get to know our collection!

Writing: I.R.B. Melo
Illustration: Done using Leonardo.AI by I.R.B. Melo

www.thefabulous.church

IBSN 9798328853651
1st Edition - April 2024

To our family, one and united in Jesus Christ. To Heloisa & Joao Paulo, the reason behind this collection.

I.R.B. Melo

LIFE OF OUR SAINTS

Catholic Books for Kids

About the collection

This collection aims at providing a first contact, for children and teenagers, with Catholic Saints stories. Our goal is to tell their amazing lives focusing on the heroism and the exceptional ability that they displayed walking the path to Heaven.

Signature Plan

One way to guarantee the whole collection and all our future releases is by having a Fabulous Signature Plan.
Scan below to see check our Monthly Plan:

SCAN TO FIND OUR SIGNATURE PLAN:

OR VISIT THE WEBSITE:
www.thefaboussaints.com

Once upon a time, in a small city called Wadowice in Poland, a baby boy named Karol Józef Wojtyla was born on May 18, 1920. He was the second son of Karol Wojtyla and Emilia Kaczorowska. Karol's childhood was filled with love, but also with sadness.

His mother passed away when he was just nine years old, and his older brother Edmund, a doctor, died when Karol was twelve. By the time he was twenty-one, his father had also passed away.

Despite these hardships, Karol grew up to be a kind and thoughtful boy. He loved to play soccer and enjoyed acting in plays. He made his First Holy Communion at age nine and was confirmed at eighteen. He attended the Marcin Wadowita high school and later enrolled in Jagiellonian University in Cracow to study and pursue his passion for drama.

In 1939, when Karol was nineteen, the world was plunged into World War II. The Nazi occupation forces closed the university, and Karol had to work in a quarry and later in a chemical factory to avoid being taken to Germany. Even in these difficult times, Karol felt a strong calling to serve God. In 1942, he secretly began studying for the priesthood in a clandestine seminary run by Cardinal Adam Stefan Sapieha.

9

Karol was also part of the "Rhapsodic Theatre," a secret group that performed plays to keep Polish culture alive during the war. His dedication to both his faith and his culture grew stronger every day.

11

After the war ended, Karol continued his studies and was ordained a priest on November 1, 1946. Soon after, he was sent to Rome to further his education. There, he completed his doctorate in theology with a thesis on faith in the works of St. John of the Cross.

13

During his vacations, Karol traveled to France, Belgium, and Holland to minister to Polish immigrants. When he returned to Poland in 1948, he served as a parish priest and chaplain for university students. He also continued his studies, eventually becoming a professor of moral philosophy and social ethics.

15

Karol's wisdom and kindness did not go unnoticed. On July 4, 1958, Pope Pius XII appointed him Auxiliary Bishop of Cracow. Karol was consecrated as a bishop on September 28, 1958. He worked tirelessly to support his people, especially during the difficult times under the communist government.

17

In 1964, Pope Paul VI appointed him Archbishop of Cracow, and three years later, he became a cardinal. Karol played a significant role in the Second Vatican Council, helping to shape important documents about the Church's mission in the modern world.

19

On October 16, 1978, something extraordinary happened. Karol Wojtyla was elected Pope, taking the name John Paul II. He was the first non-Italian pope in over 400 years!

21

Pope John Paul II traveled all over the world, spreading messages of love, peace, and faith. He visited 129 countries, meeting people from all walks of life and sharing the joy of the Gospel.

23

Pope John Paul II was known for his deep love for young people. He started World Youth Day, a global event that brings together millions of young Catholics to celebrate their faith. He also wrote many important documents, including encyclicals and letters, and published books sharing his thoughts and prayers.

25

He canonized many saints and beatified even more, recognizing their extraordinary lives of faith. He met with countless people, from world leaders to ordinary families, always emphasizing the importance of human dignity and the need for peace and justice.

27

Pope John Paul II's papacy was marked by his tireless efforts to bring people closer to God. He worked for the unity of Christians and reached out to people of other faiths. His teachings on the value of human life, the importance of family, and the need for forgiveness and reconciliation left a lasting impact on the world.

29

On April 2, 2005, Pope John Paul II passed away, leaving behind a legacy of love and faith. He was canonized as a saint on April 27, 2014, by Pope Francis. Today, we remember him as a joyful and courageous servant of God who inspired millions to live with hope and love.

31

O Holy Trinity, we thank you for having given to the Church Pope John Paul II, and for having made him shine with your fatherly tenderness, the glory of the Cross of Christ and the splendor of the Spirit of love.

He, trusting completely in your infinite mercy and in the maternal intercession of Mary, has shown himself in the likeness of Jesus the Good Shepherd and has pointed out to us holiness as the path to reach eternal communion with You.

Grant us, through his intercession,

according to your will, the grace that we implore, in the hope that he will soon be numbered among your saints.

Amen.

Saint John Paul II, pray for us.

33

Made in the USA
Columbia, SC
15 November 2024

46395123R00022